Dodge City Public Library
1001 N. Second Ave., Dodge City, KS

TOMATOES / TOMATES

Inés Vaughn
Traducción al español: Ma. Pilar Sanz

PowerKiDS press. & **Editorial Buenas Letras**™
New York

For Jack Power

Published in 2009 by The Rosen Publishing Group, Inc.
29 East 21st Street, New York, NY 10010

First Edition

Editor: Amelie von Zumbusch
Book Design: Kate Laczynski
Photo Researcher: Jessica Gerweck

Photo Credits: Cover, pp. 1, 8, 16, 19 Shutterstock.com; cover (texture), p. 1 © www.istockphoto.com/Stephen Rees; p. 4 Bambu Productions/Getty Images, p. 7 © www.istockphoto.com/Roberto A. Sanchez; p. 11 © Brooke Slezak/Getty Images; p. 12 © French School/Getty Images; p. 15 © AGE Fotostock; p. 20 © AFP/Getty Images.

Library of Congress Cataloging-in-Publication Data

Vaughn, Inés.
  Tomatoes = Tomates / Inés Vaughn ; traducción al español, Ma. Pilar Sanz. — 1st ed.
    p. cm. — (Native foods of Latin America)
  Includes index.
  ISBN 978-1-4358-2724-0 (library binding)
  1. Tomatoes—Juvenile literature. I. Sanz, Ma. Pilar (María Pilar) II. Title. III. Title: Tomates.
  SB349.V38 2009
  641.3'5642—dc22
                          2008023828

Manufactured in the United States of America

CONTENTS

CONTENIDO

Do you like tomatoes? Tomatoes taste great, both on their own and as part of a dish. Tomatoes first came from Latin America. In fact, many kinds of wild tomatoes still grow in South America's Andes mountains.

¿Te gustan los tomates? Los tomates son muy ricos, ya sea solos o como parte de un platillo. Los tomates son originarios de Latinoamérica. Actualmente, muchos tipos de tomates silvestres aún crecen en Los Andes, una cadena de montañas de Sudamérica.

Just as there are several kinds of wild tomatoes, there are many types of tomatoes people grow to eat. Many tomatoes are red, while others are yellow, orange, or purple. Tomatoes may be as big as oranges or as small as berries.

Además de la gran variedad de tomates silvestres, hay muchos tipos de tomates que cultivamos para comer. Muchos tomates son rojos, otros son amarillos, anaranjados o púrpura. Los tomates pueden ser tan grandes como una naranja o tan pequeños como las bayas.

7

8

Tomatoes are **related** to other important Latin American crops, such as chiles and potatoes. Most people call tomatoes vegetables. However, **scientists** point out that tomatoes are really fruits. This is because they have seeds inside them.

Los tomates están **relacionados** con otros importantes cultivos de Latinoamérica, como los chiles y las papas. Muchas personas piensan que los tomates son verduras. Sin embargo, los **científicos** nos dicen que en realidad son frutas. Esto se debe a que los tomates tienen semillas.

Scientists think that the first people to grow tomatoes were Indians living in Mexico over 1,500 years ago. The Aztecs were one group of Native Americans who grew and ate tomatoes. One Aztec food using tomatoes was a **sauce** made of tomatoes, squash seeds, and chiles.

Se piensa que grupos indígenas de México fueron los primeros en cultivar y comer tomates hace más de 1,500 años. Los aztecas fueron uno de esos grupos. Una de las comidas en las que los aztecas usaban tomates era en una **salsa** de tomates, semillas de calabaza y chiles.

In the 1500s, Spanish soldiers landed in Mexico. The Spanish fought the Native Americans and most of Latin America came under Spanish rule. The Spanish shipped tomatoes and other Native American foods to Europe. There, tomatoes were called many names, such as "love apples" and "golden apples."

Alrededor del año 1,500, los soldados españoles llegaron a México. Los españoles pelearon con los indígenas y en poco tiempo controlaron la mayor parte de Latinoamérica. Los españoles llevaron los tomates y otros alimentos a Europa. Ahí, los tomates fueron llamados "manzanas del amor" y "manzanas doradas".

Today, many dishes made with tomatoes are eaten in Latin America. *Salsa cruda*, which is served with many meals, is made from raw tomatoes, lime juice, chiles, onions, **cilantro**, and other raw foods. Raw tomatoes are also served in salads.

En Latinoamérica se usan tomates en muchos platillos. Muchos platillos se sirven con salsa cruda. Esta salsa está hecha con tomate, jugo de limón, chile, cebolla y cilantro. Los tomates crudos también se usan en las ensaladas.

Other Latin American dishes are made with cooked tomatoes. Mexico's widely-eaten *salsa de jitomate cocida* is a cooked tomato sauce. Tomatoes are **roasted** in Mexico, too. Many soups, such as the Puerto Rican *asopao de pollo* and *bacalao guisado*, use tomatoes.

Otros platillos latinoamericanos se preparan con tomates cocidos. En México, la popular salsa de jitomate es una salsa de tomates cocidos. En México, los tomates también se asan. En Puerto Rico, sopas como el asopao de pollo y el bacalao guisado también llevan tomates cocidos.

Tomatoes are eaten all over the world. For example, Italy is well known for many dishes made with tomatoes. Pasta is often served with a rich tomato sauce. Pizza, which comes from the Italian city of Naples, also uses tomato sauce.

Los tomates se comen en todo el mundo. Italia, por ejemplo, es famosa por sus platillos hechos con tomates. Con frecuencia, las pastas se sirven con una salsa espesa de tomate. Las pizzas, que vienen de la ciudad italiana de Nápoles, también llevan salsa de tomate.

In some places, tomatoes are so loved that people hold tomato **festivals**. The largest of these festivals is La Tomatina. It is held every August in the town of Buñol, Spain. More than 20,000 people gather to throw tomatoes at each other. It is lots of messy fun!

En algunos lugares los tomates son tan importantes que la gente organiza festivales para celebrar su cosecha. El más grande de estos festivales es La Tomatina que se celebra cada mes de agosto en Buñol, España. Más de 20,000 personas se reúnen en una divertida guerra de tomates. ¡Este festival es todo un revoltijo!

Tomatoes may be fun to throw, but they are even better to eat. Whether you eat them raw or cooked, as part of a Mexican salsa, or on an Italian pizza, tomatoes taste wonderful. Their bright colors even make food look more interesting. Here's to the tomato!

Debe de ser divertido aventar tomates, pero es mucho mejor comerlos. Ya sean crudos o cocidos en una salsa mexicana, o en una porción de pizza, los tomates son deliciosos. Además, su brillante color hace que cualquier comida se vea más rica. ¡Que vivan los tomates!

GLOSSARY

cilantro (sih-LAHN-troh) A plant used to flavor many Mexican dishes.

festivals (FES-tih-vulz) Days or special times of parties and feasting.

related (rih-LAYT-ed) Part of the same family.

roasted (ROHST-ed) Cooked over high heat or in an oven.

sauce (SOS) A topping served on or with food.

scientists (SY-un-tists) People who study the world.

GLOSARIO

asar Cocinar a temperatura muy alta o en un horno.

científicos (los) Personas que estudian nuestro mundo.

cilantro (el) Una planta que se usa para darle sabor a muchos platillos mexicanos.

festivales (los) Días o temporadas especiales que se usan para celebrar.

relacionados Que forman parte de la misma familia.

salsa (la) Acompañamiento líquido que se sirve con o sobre un platillo.

INDEX

ÍNDICE

WEB SITES / PÁGINAS DE INTERNET

Due to the changing nature of Internet links, PowerKids Press and Editorial Buenas Letras have developed an online list of Web sites related to the subject of this book. This site is updated regularly. Please use this link to access the list: www.powerkidslinks.com/nfla/tomato/